Sanjeev Kapoor's
KHAZANA

Seafood

In association with Alyona Kapoor

Popular Prakashan
www.popularprakashan.com

Published by
POPULAR PRAKASHAN PVT. LTD.
301, Mahalaxmi Chambers
22, Bhulabhai Desai Road
Mumbai - 400 026
for KHANA KHAZANA PUBLICATIONS PVT. LTD.

First Published 2007
Third Reprint 2014

(4071)
ISBN: 978-81-7991-323-9

Design: FourPlus Advertising Pvt. Ltd.

PRINTED IN INDIA
by Saurabh Printers Pvt. Ltd.
A-16, Sector 4, Noida

AUTHOR'S NOTE

"Fish is held out to be one of the greatest luxuries of the table and not only necessary, but even indispensable at all dinners where there is any pretence of excellence or fashion."

This statement by Isabella Beeton, a doyenne of the culinary world, would be heartily endorsed by lovers of seafood, who would consider a meal without fish to be incomplete and absolutely without distinction.

Gustatory pleasures apart, conventional wisdom has it that fish is excellent brain food. While there may not be much scientific data to support this belief, fish, which is high in protein, vitamins and minerals and has no saturated fats, is definitely good for your heart! Omega-3 fatty acids in oily fish (such as mackerels and sardines) are believed to reduce the risk of blood clots and thus lessen the chance of a heart attack. Doctors now recommend that one should eat two servings or more of fish a week. It would be good to remember though, that some seafood like shellfish are high in cholesterol.

If the health benefits were not enough to entice you, the legendary aphrodisiac properties of certain seafood might! The ancient world believed seafood had aphrodisiac qualities because Aphrodite, the Greek goddess of love was born of sea foam. Oysters, in particular, with their voluptuous flesh, have earned the reputation of being the ultimate aphrodisiac and food of love.

Seafood has also been considered one of the original fast foods – easy and quick to cook in a number of different ways. Fried, grilled, steamed or curried, no matter how humble, any fruit of the sea adds variety, nutrition and enjoyment to a meal.

In this book, I have included recipes that will delight your family and your guests. There are recipes for every course and for every occasion and from within our own regionally and culturally diverse country and abroad. Try out the hearty Prawn Chowder or the intriguing Angoori Prawns. The all-time favourites, Prawn Cocktail and Tandoori Pomfret have been featured as well as the more exotic Baked Fish in Chilli Coconut Sauce. There is the pride of Bengali cuisine, Bhapa Ilish and Goa's ubiquitous Fish Curry. And for those special celebrations try a Pepper-Garlic Lobster or a creamy Seafood Risotto. As always, every recipe has been tried and tested and written in a way that you will find easy to follow with never-fail results.

So cast your net wide in this book and haul in a rich catch of fresh ideas for meals rich with the treasures of the sea!

Here are some tips on buying and handling seafood.

Buying

- Fish that smells fishy is not fresh! Buy fish that is firm to the touch. If buying whole fish, look for shiny bright skin, bright eyes and moist, red gills.
- Fish fillets and steaks should have a bright, translucent quality and look moist. Avoid any seafood that looks dull, dry or opaque.
- Some shellfish, such as lobsters, crabs, crayfish, mussels, clams and oysters must be alive when purchased, unless they are frozen. The shells of clams, oysters and mussels should be tightly closed and undamaged. Prawns should not smell of ammonia or have black spots.

Storage

- Refrigerate fish as soon as possible. Fish is best eaten on the day of purchase. The optimum temperature for storage of fish is 0° Celsius. Store fish in a freezer.
- Thaw frozen fish overnight in the refrigerator. Do not thaw fish at room temperature. Cook immediately after thawing.

Cleaning and Preparation

Fish

It is best to ask your fishmonger to clean and prepare fish as it can be a very messy process. Scrape off any scales with a sharp knife. Remove the gills through the gill flaps. Cut off the fins with a sharp knife or a pair of kitchen scissors. Slit open the stomach and remove the viscera. Rinse inside and out under cold running water.

Prawns or shrimp.

Remove the head, shell and the legs. Look for the dark, thin line or vein that runs down the back of the shrimp. With a thin, sharp knife make a shallow cut along one side of the thin dark vein that runs along the back. Run the tip of the knife down the length of the vein to remove it.

Clams and Mussels

Just before cooking, soak clams or mussels for 20 minutes in fresh water. As they breathe they filter water and push salt water and sand out of their shells. Lift them out of the water and use a stiff brush to remove any additional sand or other attachments.

To open clams or mussels, prise open with the tip of a sharp pointed knife, twisting to force the shells apart. Or blanch in boiling water for 5 minutes or till they open. Discard any that do not open.

Crabs

With your thumb or the tip of a knife, lift off the apron flap on the underside of the crab. Remove the shell and the grey feathery gills (sometimes referred to as "dead men's fingers"!) and the viscera (the semi-liquid material in the body cavity). Break the body in half lengthways and twist off the legs and claws. Crack the shell of each leg or claw to remove the meat inside more easily.

Squid

Gently pull the squid's head from the body together with the viscera. Cut the tentacles just above the eyes. Pull out the hard bendable quill of a backbone and discard. Rinse the squid under cold running water.

To Get Rid of Fishy Odours

- on your fingers: rub your hands with a freshly cut lemon.
- in pans: brew some tea for ten to fifteen minutes in the pan and pour it out.
- in the house: leave a bowl of vinegar in the room overnight or for at least six hours. To hasten the process, heat the vinegar in a bowl over a pan of boiling water and turn off the heat. The vinegary vapours should get rid of the smells

Happy Cooking!

CONTENTS

MAIN COURSE - INDIAN

MAIN COURSE - INTERNATIONAL

SOUR AND SPICY PRAWN SOUP

Ingredients

- 12-16 (150 grams) medium prawns
- 4 cups Chicken Stock (page 12)
- 1 inch ginger, sliced
- 2 green chillies, roughly chopped
- 2 one-inch lemon grass stalks, roughly chopped
- 1 teaspoon lemon rind
- 3 Kaffir lime leaves
- 6-8 fresh button mushrooms, sliced
- ½ tablespoon fish sauce (optional)
- 2 tablespoons lemon juice
- salt to taste
- 1 fresh red chilli, cut into slivers
- 2 tablespoons fresh coriander leaves, roughly chopped
- 2-3 small spring onions, coarsely chopped

Method

1 Peel and devein prawns. Reserve the prawn heads and shells.

2 Pour chicken stock into a large deep pan. Add prawn shells, ginger, green

chillies, lemon grass, lemon rind and Kaffir lime leaves. Bring to a boil, cover, lower heat and simmer for fifteen minutes. Strain the mixture and return the strained stock to the pan; bring to a boil again.

3 Add prawns and button mushrooms. Simmer for two to three minutes, and stir in the fish sauce and lemon juice. Add salt to taste, stir and immediately remove from heat to prevent overcooking the prawns.

4 Serve piping hot, garnished with fresh red chilli, coriander leaves and spring onions.

CHICKEN STOCK

Boil 200 grams chicken bones in water for 5 minutes. Drain and discard water.

Boil blanched bones with a roughly chopped carrot, celery stalk and leek, 2-3 parsley stalks, 6-7 black peppercorns, 5-6 cloves, 1 bay leaf and 10 cups of water.

Remove any scum which rises to the surface and replace it with more cold water. Simmer the stock for at least one hour.

Remove from heat, strain, cool and store in a refrigerator till further use.

SEAFOOD SOUP

Ingredients

- 16 (150 grams) small prawns, peeled and deveined
- 1 (200grams) small black pomfret, skinned and filleted
- 1 small squid
- 5 cups Vegetable Stock (page 14)
- 1 lemon grass stalk, sliced diagonally
- 1 inch celery stalk, chopped
- 1 inch ginger, grated
- 4 medium fresh button mushrooms, thinly sliced
- salt to taste
- ¼ teaspoon black pepper powder
- 2 fresh red chillies, thinly sliced
- 2 stalks spring onion greens, sliced
- ½ teaspoon lemon juice

Method

1 Cut fish fillets into half-inch cubes. Clean, wash and cut squid into rings.

2 Blanch prawns, fish and squid in three to four cups of boiling salted water for one minute. Drain, refresh in cold water and set aside.

3 Bring vegetable stock to a boil in a wok. Lower heat, add lemon grass, celery, ginger, mushrooms, salt and pepper and simmer for two to three minutes.

4 Add the blanched seafood and fresh red chillies; cover and simmer for another two minutes.

5 Stir in the spring onion greens and lemon juice. Adjust seasoning, stir and simmer for one more minute.

6 Pour into soup bowls and serve hot.

VEGETABLE STOCK

Simmer 1 sliced onion, ½ sliced carrot, 2-3inch celery stalk, 1 bay leaf, 5-6 black peppercorns, 2-3 cloves and 5 cups of water for fifteen minutes. Strain.

SEAFOOD SALAD

Ingredients

- 1 cup (200grams) prawns
- ½ cup (100 grams) shrimps (small prawns)
- ½ cup mussels, cleaned and boiled
- 2 (400grams each) seer fish (*surmai*) fillets, poached
- 1 tablespoon French mustard
- 7-8 black peppercorns, crushed
- salt to taste
- 2 tablespoons lemon juice
- ¼ cup olive oil
- 10-15 iceberg lettuce leaves
- 2 tablespoons fresh parsley, chopped

Method

1 Peel, devein and boil prawns and shrimp. Cut the poached fish into one-inch pieces.

2 Mix together the French mustard, three-fourths of the crushed peppercorns, salt and lemon juice in a bowl. Add the olive oil, a little at a time, and whisk well.

3 Mix the prawns, shrimps, mussels and fish in a bowl. Add most of the dressing and toss to mix.

4 Arrange lettuce leaves in a serving plate; sprinkle with remaining crushed peppercorns. Heap the seafood salad in the centre of the lettuce leaves. Pour the rest of the dressing over.

5 Serve chilled, garnished with chopped parsley.

CHEF'S TIP

Use fillets of any fleshy fish for this salad.

FISH AND DILL SALAD

Ingredients

- 250 grams fish fillets
- a few sprigs of fresh dill leaves, roughly chopped
- 4-5 black peppercorns
- 1 bay leaf
- 2 inch celery stalk, roughly chopped
- 1 tablespoon lemon juice

salt to taste

¼ tsp black peppercorns, crushed

2 tablespoons olive oil

1 medium green capsicum, cut into half-inch diamonds

Method

1 Cut fish fillets into one-inch pieces.

2 Bring a little water to a boil in a shallow pan; add peppercorns, bay leaf and celery.

3 Add fish and cook, uncovered, for two minutes or till the fish is just done. Remove from the water carefully and set aside to cool.

4 For the dressing, combine lemon juice, salt, crushed peppercorns and olive oil in a bowl. Add dill leaves, reserving some for garnishing.

5 Place the poached fish cubes carefully in a bowl. Add the capsicum and pour the dressing over. Mix gently and serve chilled, garnished with reserved dill leaves.

CHEF'S TIP

Do not overcook the fish or it will lose its delicate texture and flavour.

PRAWN CHOWDER

Ingredients

- 16-20 (150 grams) small prawns, peeled and deveined
- ½ cup (150 grams) cream-style sweet corn
- 4 medium potatoes, quartered
- 1 medium onion, quartered
- 2 inch celery stalk, roughly broken
- salt to taste
- 1 small green capsicum, cut into small pieces
- 1 teaspoon black peppercorns, crushed

Prawn Stock

- 10-12 prawn heads and shells
- 1 bay leaf
- 5-6 black peppercorns
- 2 inch celery stalk, roughly broken
- 1 medium onion, quartered
- ½ medium carrot, sliced

Method

1 To make the prawn stock, clean, wash and roast prawn heads in a preheated grill for eight to ten minutes.

2 Place in a thick-bottomed pan with the shells, bay leaf, peppercorns, celery, onion and carrot. Add five cups of water and bring the stock to a boil. Lower heat, cover and simmer for eight to ten minutes. Strain through a piece of muslin.

3 Cook potatoes, onion, celery, half the sweet corn, two cups of prawn stock and salt in a pan till done. Strain and reserve the cooking liquid. Cool and process the solids in a blender with enough reserved liquid, till smooth.

4 Transfer the potato mixture back to the pan; add the remaining stock, capsicum and remaining sweet corn. Cover and cook on low heat for two minutes.

5 Add prawns and continue to cook for another two minutes.

6 Add crushed peppercorns, adjust seasoning and cook for one minute.

7 Pour into individual soup bowls and serve hot with breadsticks.

PRAWN COCKTAIL

Ingredients

16 (250 grams) medium prawns, peeled and deveined

1 teaspoon vinegar

salt to taste

2 hardboiled eggs, peeled and quartered

1 head of lettuce

Cocktail Sauce

3 tablespoons Mayonnaise (page 22)

2 teaspoons tomato ketchup

1 teaspoon Worcestershire sauce

1 teaspoon Tabasco sauce

1 teaspoon cream

1 tablespoon brandy (optional)

¼ teaspoon white pepper powder

Method

1 Chill four cocktail glasses in the refrigerator.

2 Heat some water in a pan with the vinegar and salt. Add prawns and cook on medium heat for two minutes. Remove and set aside to cool. Reserve

four whole prawns for garnishing and cut the remaining into half-inch pieces.

3 Shred the outer leaves of the lettuce, reserving the hearts (innermost small leaves) for garnishing.

4 For the cocktail sauce, combine the mayonnaise, tomato ketchup, Worcestershire sauce, Tabasco sauce, cream and brandy. Add the white pepper powder and salt to taste.

5 Mix the poached prawns into the cocktail sauce.

6 Line the chilled glasses with shredded lettuce. Spoon the prawn mixture into the glasses and garnish with quarters of hardboiled egg and lettuce leaves. Place a whole prawn on the rim of each glass. Serve thoroughly chilled.

MAYONNAISE

Place 1 egg yolk, salt, ¼ teaspoon white pepper powder, ¼ teaspoon mustard powder, ¼ teaspoon sugar and 1 teaspoon of vinegar in a clean bowl and mix thoroughly with a whisk. Alternatively, process the mixture in a blender.

Add 1 cup of oil, a little at a time, whisking or blending continuously, until all the oil is incorporated.

Add 1 teaspoon lemon juice and adjust seasoning.

GOLDEN FRIED JUMBO PRAWNS

Ingredients

12-16 (470grams) jumbo prawns
4-6 garlic cloves, ground
2 tablespoons oyster sauce (optional)
1 tablespoon lemon juice
1 teaspoon soy sauce
½ teaspoon white pepper powder
¼ teaspoon MSG (optional)
salt to taste
¾ cup refined flour (*maida*)
½ cup cornflour
¼ teaspoon baking powder
¾ cup oil + for deep-frying

Method

1 Peel and devein prawns, leaving the tails on.

2 Mix garlic paste, oyster sauce, lemon juice, soy sauce, white pepper powder, MSG and salt to taste. Mix in the prawns and set aside to marinate for two hours, preferably in the refrigerator.

3 Mix refined flour, cornflour, baking powder, three-fourth cup of oil, salt to

taste and three-fourth cup of water. Whisk thoroughly to make a batter of pouring consistency; set aside for twenty minutes.

4 Heat oil in a wok. Dip marinated prawns in the batter and deep-fry on medium heat, turning frequently, for two to three minutes or until crisp and golden brown. Drain on absorbent paper.

5 Serve hot with any sauce.

CHEF'S TIP

For a crisper result, increase the quantity of oil in the batter. Whisk well to incorporate the oil thoroughly.

BUTTERFLY PRAWNS

Ingredients

- 12 (350 grams) jumbo prawns
- 1 teaspoon ginger paste
- 1 teaspoon garlic paste
- 2 tablespoons soy sauce
- ¾ teaspoon black pepper powder
- 2 tablespoons cornflour
- salt to taste
- 2 eggs
- ½ cup breadcrumbs
- oil for deep-frying
- 4-5 lettuce leaves, shredded
- 2 spring onions, finely sliced

Method

1 Peel and devein prawns, leaving the tails on. Wash thoroughly, and split in half along the underside, leaving the tails firmly in place.

2 Combine prawns, ginger paste, garlic paste, soy sauce, pepper powder, cornflour and salt, and leave to marinate for ten to fifteen minutes.

3 Beat eggs lightly. Spread the breadcrumbs in a plate.

4 Heat oil in a wok. Pick up each prawn by its tail, dip in beaten egg and roll in breadcrumbs. Deep-fry till golden and drain on absorbent paper.

5 Arrange prawns on a bed of lettuce leaves and garnish with spring onions. Serve hot with Sichuan sauce.

SICHUAN SAUCE

Boil 10-12 red chillies in one cup of water for five to seven minutes. Drain, cool and grind to a fine paste.

Sauté 10 garlic cloves, 2 green chillies, 2 spring onions, all finely chopped, and 1 inch of ginger, grated, in half a cup of oil for one minute. Add the red chilli paste and sauté for a few seconds.

Add half a cup of vegetable stock, 2-3 Inches of celery, 3 tablespoons of tomato ketchup, salt, 2 teaspoon vinegar and 2 stalks spring onion greens. Simmer for one minute.

Cool and store, preferably in the refrigerator, where it will keep for about one month.

ANGOORI PRAWNS

Ingredients

- 16-20 (200 grams) prawns peeled and deveined
- 8-10 black grapes
- 8-10 red grapes
- 8-10 green grapes
- ½ cup honey
- salt to taste
- ¾ cup balsamic vinegar
- 1 teaspoon red chilli flakes
- 2 tablespoons oil + for grilling

Method

1. Heat a pan; add the honey, salt and balsamic vinegar and mix well.
2. Stir in the red chilli flakes, remove from heat and keep warm.
3. Thread the prawns and grapes onto skewers in the following order: black grape, prawn, red grape and finally green grape.
4. Season with salt and cook on an oiled grill, basting with oil and turning frequently, so that the prawns cook evenly on all sides.
5. Arrange the prawns and grapes on a platter. Pour the sauce over and serve hot.

FISH PEPPER FRY

Ingredients

- 8 (125 grams each) pomfret fillets
- 10-15 black peppercorns, crushed
- salt to taste
- 2 lemons
- ¾ cup refined flour (*maida*)
- 1 egg
- ¾ cup cornmeal (*makai ka atta*)
- oil for frying

Method

1 Sprinkle fish fillets with salt and the juice of one lemon.

2 Mix together refined flour, salt, egg and juice of the remaining lemon. Add enough water to make a thick batter.

3 Coat fish with the batter and set aside to marinate for half an hour.

4 Mix together cornmeal and crushed black peppercorns.

5 Heat oil in a shallow frying pan. Coat pomfret fillets with cornmeal mixture on both sides, shaking off excess cornmeal.

6 Shallow or deep-fry till golden brown. Drain on absorbent paper. Serve hot.

PRAWN VARUVAL

Ingredients

12-16 (150 grams) medium prawns, peeled and deveined

1 inch ginger, peeled

6-8 garlic cloves, peeled

1 teaspoon cumin powder

1 tablespoon tamarind pulp

2 tablespoons red chilli powder

½ teaspoon turmeric powder

salt to taste

2 tablespoons rice flour

¼ cup oil

1 tablespoon lemon juice

Method

1 Grind ginger and garlic to a fine paste.

2 Mix ginger-garlic paste with cumin powder, tamarind pulp, chilli powder, turmeric powder, salt, rice flour and two tablespoons of oil.

3 Marinate prawns in this mixture for at least two hours, preferably in the refrigerator.

4 Heat remaining oil in a pan; add the marinated prawns and cook for one minute on high heat. Turn the prawns over and cook for another minute.

5 Lower heat and cook for two to three minutes, turning the prawns occasionally to cook evenly.

6 Drain on absorbent paper, sprinkle with lemon juice and serve hot.

CHEF'S TIP

Varuvals are spicy Chettinad "dry-fry" dishes.

SALT AND PEPPER PRAWNS

Ingredients

- 450 grams king prawns
- salt to taste
- 1 teaspoon black pepper powder
- 10 black peppercorns, crushed
- 3 tablespoons cornflour
- 3 tablespoons soy sauce
- 2 tablespoons oil for deep-frying
- 5 garlic cloves, crushed
- 1 inch ginger, chopped
- 2 spring onions, sliced
- a pinch of MSG (optional)
- 4 stalks spring onion greens, sliced

Method

1. Peel and devein prawns, leaving the tails on, and wash thoroughly.

2. Mix salt, half a teaspoon of black pepper powder, half the crushed peppercorns, two tablespoons of cornflour and one tablespoon of soy sauce in a bowl.

3. Add the prawns, mix well and marinate for fifteen minutes. Mix

remaining cornflour and three tablespoons of water.

4 Heat oil in a wok and deep-fry the prawns for two minutes. Drain on absorbent paper.

5 In a separate wok, heat two tablespoons of oil; add garlic, ginger and spring onions and sauté for two minutes on high heat.

6 Add the prawns, salt, remaining black pepper powder, half the remaining crushed peppercorns, remaining soy sauce, MSG, cornflour mixture and spring onion greens.

7 Stir-fry on high heat for four minutes, or until the prawns are cooked through.

8 Sprinkle with the remaining crushed peppercorns and serve hot.

PRAWNS IN GARLIC BUTTER

Ingredients

- 400 grams prawns, peeled and deveined
- 25-30 garlic cloves
- 4 tablespoons butter
- 1 tablespoon mustard paste
- 1 tablespoon lemon juice
- 8-10 black peppercorns, crushed
- salt to taste
- a few sprigs of fresh parsley, finely chopped

Method

1. Peel, wash and grind garlic to a paste.
2. Heat butter in a pan and fry garlic paste for a few seconds.
3. Add prawns, mustard paste, lemon juice, crushed peppercorns and salt.
4. Simmer, uncovered, on low heat till prawns are cooked.
5. Sprinkle with chopped parsley and serve hot.

MALVANI PRAWN FRY

Ingredients

- 300 grams medium prawns, peeled and deveined
- salt to taste
- 1½ tablespoons lemon juice
- ¾ teaspoon turmeric powder
- 3 teaspoons red chilli powder
- 1½ teaspoons ginger paste
- 1½ teaspoons garlic paste
- oil for shallow-frying
- 4 tablespoons rice flour
- 4 tablespoons semolina (*rawa/sooji*)

Method

1 Wash prawns under running water, drain and pat dry. Marinate in salt and lemon juice for fifteen minutes.

2 Mix together turmeric powder, chilli powder, salt, ginger paste and garlic paste. Marinate prawns in this mixture, covered, for thirty minutes, preferably in a refrigerator.

3 Heat oil in a flat griddle (*tawa*). Mix rice flour and semolina and spread on a plate. Roll the prawns in this mixture and shallow-fry till golden on both sides.

4 Drain on absorbent paper and serve hot.

TANDOORI POMFRET

Ingredients

- 2 (300 grams each) pomfrets
- salt to taste
- 2 tablespoons lemon juice
- 1 inch ginger, peeled
- 5-6 garlic cloves, peeled
- ½ teaspoon carom seeds (*ajwain*)
- ¾ cup yogurt, whisked
- 1 egg, beaten
- 2 tablespoons gram flour (*besan*)
- ½ teaspoon turmeric powder
- 1 teaspoon *garam masala* powder
- 2 tablespoons butter or oil

Method

1 Gut and wash the pomfrets. Make incisions on both sides and rub in salt and lemon juice. Set aside for twenty minutes.

2 Grind ginger and garlic to a fine paste.

3 Combine the ginger-garlic paste, carom seeds, yogurt, egg, gram flour, turmeric powder and *garam masala*.

Rub the mixture over the fish and leave to marinate for about one hour in the refrigerator.

4 Thread each pomfret onto a skewer and cook in a moderately hot *tandoor* for about eight to ten minutes.

5 Baste with butter or oil and cook for another three minutes.

6 Serve hot with lemon wedges.

CHEF'S TIP

Tandoori Pomfret can also be cooked in a preheated oven at 180°C.

PRAWN OLIVETTI

Ingredients

12-16 (200grams) medium prawns
12-16 green olives, stoned
2 spring onions
2 teaspoons ginger paste
2 teaspoons garlic paste
1 teaspoon red chilli powder
½ teaspoon black pepper powder
4 teaspoons balsamic vinegar
salt to taste
1 tablespoon oil + for brushing
½ teaspoon crushed red chillies
1 teaspoon fresh thyme, chopped
10-12 cherry tomatoes, halved
10-12 fresh button mushrooms, quartered
2 tablespoons olive oil
6-8 lettuce leaves
4-5 black peppercorns, crushed
sprigs of fresh parsley, to garnish

Method

1 Peel and devein prawns, leaving the tails on. Slice the spring onion bulbs and greens separately.

2 Mix ginger paste, garlic paste, chilli powder, black pepper powder, balsamic vinegar, salt and one tablespoon of oil in a bowl.

3 Add the prawns, crushed red chillies and fresh thyme. Marinate prawns for half an hour in the refrigerator.

4 Thread an olive between two prawns onto a toothpick.

5 Add the cherry tomatoes, mushrooms and the spring onion greens to the leftover marinade.

6 Brush prawns with a little oil and grill till evenly cooked.

7 In the meanwhile, heat olive oil in a pan. Add the sliced spring onions and sauté for a few seconds. Add the vegetables with the marinade and cook on high heat for a minute or two.

8 Add the grilled prawns to the vegetable sauce and mix in the crushed peppercorns.

9 Arrange lettuce leaves on a serving plate.

10 Spoon prawns and vegetables over the lettuce and garnish with fresh parsley. Serve at once.

FISH CAKES

Ingredients

- 500 grams seer fish (*surmai*), thickly sliced
- salt to taste
- 8 black peppercorns
- 1 large potato, boiled and mashed
- 3 eggs
- 4 garlic cloves, finely chopped
- ½ inch ginger, finely chopped
- 4 green chillies, finely chopped
- 1 tablespoon lemon juice
- 1 medium onion, finely chopped
- a few sprigs of fresh coriander leaves, finely chopped
- breadcrumbs
- oil for shallow-frying

Method

1 In a shallow pan, cook fish in one cup of water with salt and peppercorns till all the water has evaporated. Leave to cool and carefully remove the skin and bones. Mash the fish with a fork.

2 Mix the mashed fish with the mashed potato, one egg, garlic, ginger, green

chillies, lemon juice, onion and coriander leaves.

3 Divide the mixture into twelve equal portions and shape into flat, oval cakes.

4 Beat the remaining eggs. Dip each fish cake in the beaten eggs and roll in the breadcrumbs.

5 Heat oil in a frying pan on medium heat and shallow-fry fish cakes till golden brown on both sides.

6 Drain on absorbent paper and serve hot.

CHEF'S TIP

To make prawn cakes, replace fish with peeled and deveined prawns.

AMRITSARI MACHCHI

Ingredients

- 600 grams fish fillets (preferably *surmai*)
- ½ cup malt vinegar
- 1 cup gram flour (*besan*)
- ½ cup yogurt
- salt to taste
- 1 egg
- 1 tablespoon lemon juice
- 1 tsp carom seeds (*ajwain*)
- 1 tablespoon red chilli powder
- 2 tablespoons ginger paste
- 2 tablespoons garlic paste
- oil for deep-frying
- 1 teaspoon *chaat masala*
- 6-8 lemon wedges

Method

1 Clean, wash and cut fish into one-and-a-half inch cubes. Marinate in vinegar for twenty minutes. Drain and pat fish dry.

2 Make a batter of *besan*, yogurt, salt, egg, lemon juice, *ajwain*, chilli powder, ginger and garlic pastes.

3 Marinate the fish in the batter for about twenty minutes.

4 Heat oil in a *kadai* and deep-fry the fish till golden brown and crisp.

5 Sprinkle with *chaat masala* and serve hot with lemon wedges.

CHEF'S TIP

You can use any plain vinegar in place of malt vinegar

BHAPA ILISH

Ingredients

500 grams hilsa (*ilish*), sliced
salt to taste
1 teaspoon turmeric powder
1 teaspoon yellow mustard seeds
1 teaspoon black mustard seeds
2-3 green chillies
1 inch ginger, sliced
3 tablespoons mustard oil

Method

1 Sprinkle fish slices with salt and half the turmeric powder.

2 Make a smooth paste of yellow mustard seeds, black mustard seeds, green chillies, ginger, salt and remaining turmeric powder.

3 Place the fish in a pan that will fit into a pressure cooker. Spread paste liberally all over fish. Pour mustard oil on top.

4 Place a trivet or ring in the pressure cooker. Pour three cups of water into the cooker and place the pan with the fish on the trivet. Cover the cooker with the lid and steam the fish for eight to ten minutes. Serve hot.

MACHER JHOL

Ingredients

1	whole small fish (preferably *rohu*)
2	teaspoons turmeric powder
	salt to taste
2	medium potatoes
1½	tablespoons coriander seeds
1	teaspoon cumin seeds
3	tablespoons mustard oil
¼	teaspoon onion seeds (*kalonji*)
5	green chillies, slit

Method

1 Remove the head, gut the fish and wash thoroughly. Cut into half-inch thick slices across the bone (darnes). Pat the slices dry with a kitchen towel and apply salt and turmeric powder.

2 Wash, peel and cut potatoes into half-inch thick fingers.

3 Dry-roast coriander and cumin seeds and grind with a little water to a fine paste.

4 Heat two-tablespoons of mustard oil in a pan till it reaches smoking point. Remove from heat and set aside to cool.

5 Reheat the oil on medium heat. Add a few slices of fish at a time and fry for one minute on each side. Drain on absorbent paper.

6 Add potato fingers to the pan and sauté for two to three minutes. Heat the remaining oil in the same pan, add *kalonji* and slit green chillies and sauté for a few minutes.

7 Add the ground coriander-cumin paste and cook on low heat for one minute, sprinkling a little water, if required.

8 Add two-cups of water, the sautéed potatoes and salt and simmer for four to five minutes, or until the potatoes are completely cooked.

9 Gently slide the fried fish into the pan and simmer for two to three minutes, or until the fish is cooked through. Serve hot with steamed rice.

PRAWN GHASSI

Ingredients

18-20 (300grams) medium prawns, peeled and deveined

salt to taste

1 cup grated fresh coconut

2 medium onions, peeled and chopped

4 dried red chillies, roasted

2 teaspoons coriander seeds

1 teaspoon cumin seeds

8-10 black peppercorns

¼ teaspoon fenugreek seeds (*methi dana*)

½ teaspoon turmeric powder

5 garlic cloves, peeled

1½ tablespoons tamarind pulp

3 tablespoons oil

Method

1 Wash prawns thoroughly under running water. Drain and pat dry. Sprinkle with salt and set aside for one hour, preferably in the refrigerator.

2 Grind grated coconut, half the chopped onions, red chillies, coriander

seeds, cumin seeds, peppercorns, fenugreek seeds, turmeric powder, garlic and tamarind pulp with enough water to a smooth paste.

3 Heat oil in a *kadai* and fry the remaining chopped onions till light brown.

4 Add the *masala* paste and sauté for two to three minutes. Add two cups of water and mix well. When the mixture comes to a boil add prawns and adjust seasoning.

5 Simmer for five minutes. Serve hot.

CHEF'S TIP

Always cover fish or shellfish with a tight-fitting lid while marinating in a refrigerator to prevent other foods from absorbing the strong odours.

CLAMS IN COCONUT GRAVY

Ingredients

- 2 cups (400 grams) clams (*tisrai*)
- salt to taste
- ½ tablespoon lemon juice
- ½ cup grated fresh coconut
- 3 tablespoons oil
- 2 medium onions, finely chopped
- 1 tablespoon ginger paste
- 1 tablespoon garlic paste
- ¼ teaspoon turmeric powder
- ½ tablespoon tamarind pulp
- a few sprigs of fresh coriander leaves, chopped

Masala

- 1 tablespoon oil
- 2 medium onions, thinly sliced
- 5-6 cloves
- 7-8 black peppercorns
- 2 one-inch cinnamon sticks
- ½ teaspoon caraway seeds (*shahi jeera*)

1 teaspoon coriander seeds

5-6 dried red chillies

¼ cup grated dried coconut

Method

1 Clean and wash clams thoroughly. Prise open the shell and break off one half of the shell, leaving the clam meat on the other half shell. Apply salt and lemon juice and set aside for fifteen minutes.

2 For the *masala*, sauté sliced onion in one tablespoon of oil till golden brown.

3 Dry-roast cloves, peppercorns, cinnamon, caraway seeds, coriander seeds, red chillies and dried coconut separately. Grind the roasted spices with browned onions and one-fourth cup of water to a very fine paste.

4 Add half a cup of warm water to the grated fresh coconut. Grind and squeeze out the thick milk.

5 Heat three tablespoons of oil in a pan; add chopped onion, and sauté till light golden brown.

6 Add ginger paste and garlic paste and sauté for a few seconds. Add the ground *masala*, and sauté on low heat for two to three minutes. Add one-and-a half

cups of water and bring the mixture to a boil.

7 Add the clams, turmeric powder, coconut milk and tamarind pulp and cook, covered, for five to seven minutes.

8 Garnish with chopped coriander leaves and serve with steamed rice.

CHEF'S TIP

To open clams easily, blanch in plenty of boiling water for five minutes till they open. Discard any clams that do not open.

PRAWN BALCHAO

Ingredients

- 2¼ cups (450 grams) prawns, peeled and deveined
- salt to taste
- 2 one-inch pieces ginger, roughly chopped
- 15-20 garlic cloves, roughly chopped
- 1 teaspoon cumin seeds
- 12-15 dried red chillies
- 10-12 cloves
- 2 one-inch cinnamon sticks
- 1 teaspoon mustard seeds
- 1 cup malt vinegar
- ¾ cup oil
- 2 large onions, finely chopped
- 4 large tomatoes, chopped
- 2 tablespoons sugar

Method

1 Wash the prawns thoroughly. Drain excess water and pat dry with a

kitchen towel. Sprinkle with salt and set aside.

2 Grind ginger, garlic, cumin seeds, red chillies, cloves, cinnamon and mustard seeds with vinegar to a fine paste.

3 Heat oil in a *kadai* and sauté the prawns till the moisture dries up. Remove prawns and set aside. In the same oil, sauté onions till soft and light brown.

4 Add chopped tomatoes and cook on high heat till thick and pulpy and the oil separates.

5 Add the ground *masala* and stir-fry for two to three minutes. Add the prawns and sugar. Check seasoning and cook on low heat for five to seven minutes more or till the oil separates.

6 Serve hot with *pao* or steamed rice.

CHEF'S TIP

You need not use large prawns for this dish as Prawn Balchao tastes better made with small prawns or shrimp. And it is less expensive too!

GOAN FISH CURRY

Ingredients

- 2 (400 grams each) pomfrets, or any other flat fish
- 2 teaspoons cumin seeds
- 2 tablespoons coriander seeds
- 6 dried red chillies
- ½ cup grated fresh coconut
- 2 inches ginger, chopped
- 15 garlic cloves, chopped
- 2 tablespoons tamarind pulp
- 2 tablespoons oil
- 1 small onion, chopped
- 2 green chillies, slit and halved
- salt to taste
- 1 tablespoon malt vinegar

Method

1. Clean, wash and cut each pomfret into five or six pieces.
2. Dry-roast cumin seeds, coriander seeds and red chillies.

3 Grind the roasted spices along with grated coconut, ginger, garlic, tamarind and a little water to a fine paste.

4 Spread half the ground paste over the fish.

5 Heat oil in a pan; add chopped onions and sauté till golden brown. Add green chillies and cook on medium heat for three minutes, stirring continuously.

6 Add the remaining ground paste and stir well. Sauté for five minutes.

7 Add one-and-a-half cups of water, stir well and bring the curry to a boil; add the marinated fish and salt. Cook on low heat for about five minutes or till the fish is just done.

8 Stir in vinegar and serve hot with steamed rice.

CHEF'S TIP

You can make a meal of steamed rice and fish curry. Fish curry tastes best with Goan parboiled rice, which has small, round reddish grains and a nutty flavour.

CRAB MASALA

Ingredients

- 6 (180 grams each) crabs
- 2 tablespoons oil
- 2 bay leaves
- 3-4 black peppercorns
- 2 cloves
- 2 green cardamoms
- 4-5 medium onions, finely chopped
- ½ teaspoon turmeric powder
- ½-1 teaspoon red chilli powder

Green Masala

- ½ medium bunch (125 grams) fresh coriander leaves
- 4-5 green chillies
- 2 tablespoons grated ginger
- 2 tablespoons grated garlic
- 2 cloves
- 6 black peppercorns
- ½ inch cinnamon

Coconut Masala

- 2 tablespoons oil
- 1 tablespoon coriander seeds
- 2 black peppercorns
- 2 cloves
- 1 inch cinnamon
- 1 medium onion, sliced
- 1½ cups grated fresh coconut

Method

1 Separate the claws and cut the crabs into two. Wash and remove gills and stomach sac. Crack the claws lightly.

2 Grind all the ingredients for the green *masala* with approximately one tablespoon of water to a fine paste.

3 For the coconut *masala,* heat two tablespoons of oil in a pan. Add coriander seeds, peppercorns, cloves and cinnamon and sauté for two minutes. Add onion and continue to sauté till onion turns pink.

4 Add the coconut and continue to sauté on very low heat till the coconut turns brown, making sure that it does not burn. Cool and grind to a very fine paste with half a cup of water.

5 Heat two tablespoons of oil in a *kadai.* Add bay leaves, peppercorns, cloves and green cardamoms, and sauté for two

minutes. Add the green *masala* and sauté till fragrant. Add onions and sauté till golden brown.

6 Add turmeric powder and chilli powder and sauté for a couple of minutes more.

7 Add the crabs and mix well. Add one cup of water and salt to taste, bring to a boil, lower heat and simmer till the crabs are cooked.

8 Stir in the coconut *masala* and half a cup of water. When the gravy comes to a boil, remove from heat and leave to stand, covered, for about five minutes.

9 Serve hot with steamed rice or *chapaatis*.

CHEF'S TIP

The colour of crabs changes to a bright orangey-red when cooked.

PATRANI MACHCHI

Ingredients

- 8 (125 grams each) pomfret fillets
- salt to taste
- ¼ cup lemon juice
- 1 cup coriander leaves
- 4 green chillies
- ½ cup grated fresh coconut
- 3 teaspoons cumin seeds
- 6-8 garlic cloves
- 4 banana leaves

Method

1. Clean, wash and cut each fish fillet in half.
2. Sprinkle with salt and half the lemon juice and set aside for half an hour.
3. Grind coriander leaves, green chillies, coconut, cumin seeds and garlic to a fine paste. Stir in salt and remaining lemon juice.
4. Marinate fish fillets in the ground paste for at least fifteen minutes.
5. Cut banana leaves into four pieces each.

6 Place a marinated piece of fish on each leaf along with a little of the marinade. Fold the leaf to cover and seal the fish fillets completely. Tie the fish parcels with a thread if necessary.

7 Steam the fish in a steamer for fifteen minutes and serve hot in the leaves.

CHEF'S TIP

To soften banana leaves and make them more pliable, pass them rapidly over an open flame.

CHINGRI MACHER PULAO

Ingredients

- 1½ cups rice, soaked
- 20-25 (200 grams) small prawns, peeled and deveined
- 1¼ teaspoons red chilli powder
- ½ teaspoon turmeric powder
- 5 tablespoons *desi ghee*
- 2 medium onions, finely chopped
- 5 garlic cloves, finely chopped
- ¾ inch ginger, finely chopped
- 3 green chillies, slit
- ½ teaspoon *paanch phoron**
- 4-5 cloves
- 6-8 black peppercorns
- 1 inch cinnamon
- ½ teaspoon mustard paste
- ¾ cup Coconut Milk (page 87)
- salt to taste
- ¾ cup green peas
- 1½ tablespoons lemon juice
- 2 small tomatoes, quartered
- a few sprigs of fresh coriander leaves, chopped

Method

1 Wash rice in two changes of water and soak in three cups of water for thirty minutes. Drain.

2 Combine chilli powder, turmeric powder and prawns and leave to marinate for half an hour, preferably in the refrigerator

3 Heat three tablespoons of *ghee* in a large pan; sauté the onions, garlic, ginger and green chillies till light brown.

4 Add *paanch phoron*, cloves, peppercorns, cinnamon and mustard paste and sauté for half a minute. Add drained rice and sauté for two to three minutes.

5 Add two-and-a-quarter cups of water, coconut milk and salt to taste. Bring the mixture to a boil, cover and cook on low heat.

6 In a separate pan, heat the remaining *ghee* and fry the prawns and peas for two to three minutes.

7 When the rice is nearly cooked, gently stir in the prawn and pea mixture, cover and cook till done.

8 Sprinkle with lemon juice and mix lightly. Serve hot, garnished with tomatoes and chopped coriander leaves.

* *Paanch phoron is a mixture of equal quantities of mustard seeds, cumin seeds, fenugreek seeds (methi dana), fennel seeds (saunf) and onion seeds (kalonji).*

TALELA BANGDA

Ingredients

- 8 medium mackerels (*bangda*)
- salt to taste
- 2 tablespoons lemon juice
- 10-12 pieces of *kokum*
- 3 teaspoons red chilli powder
- ½ teaspoon turmeric powder
- 2 tablespoons ginger paste
- 2 tablespoons garlic paste
- oil for shallow-frying
- 1 cup coarse rice powder
- lemon wedges

Method

1 Clean and gut the mackerels and wash thoroughly. Make four to five quarter-inch deep cuts on both sides, and rub in the salt and lemon juice. Set aside for fifteen minutes.

2 Soak *kokum* in half a cup of warm water for fifteen minutes; crush lightly to extract the pulp and strain.

3 Combine red chilli powder, turmeric powder, ginger paste, garlic paste, *kokum* pulp and salt; marinate mackerels in this paste for half an hour, preferably in a refrigerator.

4 Heat two tablespoons of oil in a frying pan. Roll the fish in the rice powder

and shallow-fry a few at a time for two to three minutes.

5 Turn over, drizzle with some more oil and continue to cook on medium heat for two minutes, or till the mackerels are light brown and crisp. Drain on absorbent paper.

6 Serve hot with lemon wedges.

CHEF'S TIP

If kokum is not available, use tamarind pulp instead.

MEEN POLLICHATHU

Ingredients

- 4 (250 grams each) small pomfrets
- salt to taste
- 1 teaspoon black pepper powder
- 1 teaspoon turmeric powder
- 2 tablespoons lemon juice
- 6-8 dried red chillies
- 1 inch ginger, roughly chopped
- 8-10 garlic cloves, roughly chopped
- 7-8 black peppercorns
- 2 tablespoons oil + for shallow-frying
- ½ teaspoon mustard seeds
- 10 fresh curry leaves
- 10 small onions, sliced
- 2 green chillies, slit
- 2 medium tomatoes, chopped
- ½ cup thick Coconut Milk (page 87)
- 4 banana leaves (see page 68)

Method

1 Clean and gut the fish. Make slits on both sides. Mix salt, black pepper powder, turmeric powder and lemon juice in a bowl. Spread this mixture over the fish and set aside for half an hour.

2 Grind red chillies, ginger, garlic and peppercorns to a fine paste.

3 Heat oil in a pan. Add mustard seeds, curry leaves and onions and sauté for two to three minutes. Add green chillies and *masala* paste and sauté on high heat. Add tomatoes and continue to sauté for a few minutes more.

4 Add thick coconut milk and salt to the *masala* and mix. Remove from heat and spread on a plate to cool.

5 Grease the banana leaves with a little oil. Spread some *masala* on each leaf. Place a pomfret on the *masala* and spread some more *masala* over the fish. Fold in the edges of the leaf and secure with toothpicks to seal tightly.

6 Heat some oil in a pan and place the wrapped fish in it. Cook for eight to ten minutes, turning the fish parcels a few times.

7 Serve hot in the banana leaves.

BATTER-FRIED FISH

Ingredients

- 4 (200 grams each) fish fillets
- ¾ teaspoon fresh yeast
- 2 tablespoons + ½ cup milk
- ½ cup + 6 tablespoons refined flour (*maida*)
- ½ cup cornflour
- ½ teaspoon baking powder
- salt to taste
- 1 egg yolk
- oil for deep-frying

Method

1. Sprinkle a little salt on the fish fillets.
2. Dissolve yeast in two tablespoons of warm milk. Leave in a warm place. Add salt and mix.
3. Sift together half a cup of refined flour, cornflour, baking powder and salt.
4. Mix the egg yolk into the yeast mixture.
5. Add this mixture to the flour and whisk well. Add milk and continue to whisk to make a thick, smooth batter. Cover and rest the batter for one to one-and-a-half hours to ferment slightly.

6 Heat oil in a deep-frying pan. Roll the fish fillets in the remaining flour, shaking off the excess flour. Dip the fillets in the batter and deep-fry in hot oil till golden. Drain on absorbent paper.

7 Serve hot with Tartare Sauce (see alongside).

TARTARE SAUCE

Combine 1 cup Mayonnaise (page 22), 1 tablespoon chopped fresh parsley, 1 chopped small onion, 2 tablespoons gherkins, 1 tablespoon lemon juice and salt and white pepper powder to taste.

Refrigerate for at least one hour before serving.

PEPPER-GARLIC LOBSTER

Ingredients

- 4 medium lobsters
- ½ teaspoon black peppercorns, crushed
- 14-16 garlic cloves, chopped
- 3 tablespoons lemon juice
- salt to taste
- 6-8 sprigs fresh coriander leaves
- 2 tablespoons cornflour
- 1 tablespoon oil
- 4 tablespoons butter
- 1 small onion, chopped
- 1 teaspoon sugar
- 2 cups Chicken Stock (page 12)
- ¼ teaspoon MSG (optional)

Method

1 Remove the head and shell of the lobsters. Cut each lobster into half, remove the flesh and cut into one-inch pieces.

2 Add lemon juice, half a teaspoon of salt and set aside to marinate for about half an hour.

3 Place coriander sprigs in iced water. Mix cornflour and half a cup of water.

4 Heat oil and butter together in a wok or pan. Add chopped onion and garlic and stir-fry for a few seconds.

5 Add marinated lobster, sugar and crushed peppercorns. Continue to stir-fry for one minute.

6 Stir in chicken stock and bring to a boil. Stir in salt, MSG and cornflour mixture. Cook on high heat for one minute, or until the sauce thickens and coats the lobster.

7 Serve, garnished with crisp coriander sprigs.

CHEF'S TIP

Serve lobster in cooked lobster shells to wow your guests!

BAKED FISH WITH CHILLI-COCONUT SAUCE

Ingredients

4 (200 grams each) fish fillets (such as *surmai*)

sea salt to taste

2 fresh red chillies, chopped

2 tablespoons lemon juice

2 tablespoons olive oil

a few sprigs of fresh parsley

Chilli Coconut Sauce

1 teaspoon crushed dried red chillies

1 cup Coconut Milk (page 87)

2 tablespoons butter

2 tablespoons olive oil

1 small onion, finely chopped

4 garlic cloves, finely chopped

2 inches ginger, finely chopped

1 cup fresh tomato purée

salt to taste

1½ cups Fish Stock (page 96)

2 tablespoons refined flour (*maida*)

Method

1 Preheat the oven to 220°C.

2 If the fish fillets are too long cut them into six-inch long pieces. Make criss-cross slits on each fillet. Rub with a mixture of sea salt, fresh red chillies and lemon juice.

3 Grease a baking tray. Place the fish on it and drizzle olive oil on top. Bake for twenty minutes.

4 For the sauce, heat butter and one tablespoon of olive oil in a pan. Add onion, garlic and ginger, and sauté for a few seconds. Add fresh tomato purée, salt, fish stock and crushed red chillies, and cook for about ten minutes.

5 Strain, pressing the mixture through the strainer.

6 Heat the remaining olive oil in a separate pan. Add refined flour and sauté for two minutes on low heat. Add the strained sauce and cook till thick.

7 Stir in the coconut milk and bring to a boil. Remove from heat.

8 Place the fish fillets on a serving dish and pour the sauce around it. Garnish with sprigs of parsley and serve hot.

JUMBO PRAWNS IN HONEY-CHILLI SAUCE

Ingredients

8 (250 grams) jumbo prawns
2 tablespoons cornflour
½ teaspoon black peppercorns, crushed
salt to taste
1 tablespoon soy sauce
1 teaspoon ginger paste
oil for deep-frying

Honey Chilli Sauce

2 tablespoons honey
1 teaspoon red chilli flakes
2 teaspoons red chilli sauce
2 tablespoon oil
10-12 garlic cloves, crushed
1 medium onion, chopped
¾ cup tomato ketchup
1 teaspoon soy sauce
1 teaspoon ginger paste
¼ teaspoon crushed black peppercorns

1 tablespoon lemon juice

3-4 stalks sping onion greens, roughly chopped

Method

1 Peel and devein prawns, keeping the tails intact; wash thoroughly under running water.

2 Place prawns in a bowl with the cornflour, crushed peppercorns, salt, one tablespoon soy sauce and ginger paste. Mix well and leave to marinate for fifteen minutes.

3 Heat oil in a deep pan and deep-fry the prawns for half a minute. Drain on absorbent paper.

4 For the sauce, heat two tablespoons of oil in a separate pan; add crushed garlic and sauté on high heat till slightly burnt. Add onion and sauté till soft.

5 Add the tomato ketchup, one teaspoon soy sauce, red chilli sauce, ginger paste, crushed peppercorns and red chilli flakes, and stir-fry for two minutes. Add fried prawns and stir.

6 Add the honey, salt and lemon juice and cook for one minute. Add the spring onion greens, mix and cook for one minute more. Serve hot.

PRAWNS IN THAI RED CURRY SAUCE

Ingredients

- 16 (250 grams) medium prawns, peeled and deveined
- 2 tablespoons oil
- 1 teaspoon lemon juice
- 1 teaspoon soy sauce
- 1 cup Coconut Milk (page 87)
- 6-8 fresh basil leaves

Red Curry Paste

- 1 medium onion, chopped
- 4 garlic cloves, chopped
- 8-10 dried red chillies
- 4 inch lemon grass stalk
- 2 teaspoons coriander seeds
- 1 teaspoon cumin seeds
- 6 black peppercorns
- salt to taste

Method

1 Grind the ingredients for the red curry paste with a little water to a smooth paste.

2 In a deep microwave-safe bowl, mix paste with oil and three-fourth cup of water. Cook, uncovered, on HIGH (100%) for three minutes.

3 Stir in the lemon juice, soy sauce and basil leaves. Cook, uncovered, on HIGH (100%) for one minute.

4 Mix in prawns and coconut milk and cook, covered, on HIGH (100%) for three minutes. Adjust seasoning and serve hot.

CHEF'S TIP

To extract 1 cup of coconut milk, process 1 cup of fresh grated coconut with half a cup of warm water in a blender. Press through a fine strainer or piece of muslin.

SEAFOOD RISOTTO

Ingredients

- 1 cup rice (*Surti Kolam*), soaked
- 1 (75 grams) pomfret fillet, cut into 1-inch cubes
- 12 (150 grams) medium prawns
- 7-8 (15 grams) shelled clams (*tisrai*)
- 3 tablespoons olive oil
- 1 bay leaf
- 2 small onions, chopped
- 4 garlic cloves, roughly chopped
- 3½ cups Vegetable Stock (page 14)
- ½ teaspoon dried thyme
- ¼ cup thick cream
- 2 tablespoons Parmesan cheese, grated
- salt to taste
- 5-6 black peppercorns, crushed

Method

1 Heat one tablespoon of olive oil in a pan. Sauté pomfret, prawns and clams separately for one minute each. Drain and set aside.

2 Add two tablespoons of oil to the same pan; add bay leaf, onions and garlic and sauté till lightly browned.

3 Add drained rice and sauté for two minutes. Add vegetable stock and thyme, bring the mixture to a boil, cover and cook till the rice is done.

4 Stir in the sautéed seafood, cream and Parmesan cheese. Season with salt and crushed peppercorns. Serve hot.

CHEF'S TIP

Traditionally Arborio rice is used to make risotto.

SEAFOOD AND NOODLE STIR-FRY

Ingredients

- 300 grams flat noodles
- 100 grams fish fillets, cut into1-inch pieces
- 6-8 mussels or clams (*tisrai*)
- 2 (180 grams each) medium crabs
- 12 (150 grams) small prawns, peeled and deveined
- 6 tablespoons oil
- 1 medium onion, sliced
- 6-8 garlic cloves, finely chopped
- 1 inch ginger, finely chopped
- 1 medium green capsicum, cut into thin strips
- 1 tablespoon soy sauce
- 1 tablespoon oyster sauce
- ½ teaspoon white pepper powder
- ¼ teaspoon MSG (optional)
- salt to taste
- 1 tablespoon lemon juice
- 1 stalk spring onion greens, finely shredded

Method

1 Prise open mussel or clam shells with a knife and scoop out the meat.

2 Boil crabs in water for three to four minutes. Cool, separate the claws, crack them lightly and set aside. Extract the meat from the rest of the crab.

3 Boil flat noodles in water. Drain and spread on a plate to cool.

4 Heat oil in a wok; add sliced onion, chopped garlic and ginger, and stir-fry for a few seconds.

5 Add, fish and mussels or clams, prawns and capsicum and continue to stir-fry for one minute.

6 Add boiled noodles, crab meat, crab claws, soy sauce, oyster sauce, white pepper powder, MSG and salt to taste. Cook on high heat for a couple of minutes, tossing continuously.

7 Stir in the lemon juice and serve hot, garnished with the shredded spring onion greens.

PENNE WITH SEAFOOD AND TOMATO SAUCE

Ingredients

- 4 cups penne (quill-shaped pasta)
- 8 garlic cloves, chopped
- 2 (60 grams each) pomfret fillets, cut into 1-inch cubes
- 25 (45 grams) clams (*tisrai*)
- 20 (300 grams) medium prawns, shelled and deveined
- 4 cups Tomato Concasse (page 94)
- 1 cup tomato purée
- salt to taste
- 5 tablespoons olive oil
- 3 medium onions, chopped
- 2 teaspoons red chilli flakes
- 1 teaspoon dried oregano
- 10-12 black peppercorns, crushed
- 2 tablespoons Parmesan cheese
- 1 tablespoon parsley, chopped

Method

1 Boil penne in three to four cups of water with salt till al dente (firm to the bite). Drain, refresh in cold water and drain. Stir in one tablespoon of olive oil and set aside.

2 Blanch clams in five or six cups of boiling water for five minutes or till the clams open up. Remove the flesh and set aside.

3 Heat two tablespoons of olive oil, add garlic and sauté for one minute. Add onions and sauté till lightly browned.

4 Stir in the tomato concasse and tomato purée and cook for ten to twelve minutes or till it reaches the consistency of a thick sauce. Add salt and red chilli flakes. Mix and set aside

5 Heat two tablespoons of olive oil in a pan; sauté fish cubes, prawns, and clams separately for one minute till lightly browned. Drain and set aside.

6 To the same pan, add the prepared sauce, oregano and crushed peppercorns and cook till heated through.

7 Add the cooked pasta and toss to mix. Add the sautéed seafood and toss again. Adjust the seasoning.

8 Transfer to a serving plate, sprinkle Parmesan cheese and parsley on top and serve immediately.

CHEF'S TIP

To make Tomato Concasse, blanch tomatoes in plenty of boiling water for two minutes. Drain and refresh in cold water, peel, cut in half, remove seeds and chop roughly.

GARLIC-CHILLI CRABS

Ingredients

- 2 (200 grams each) large crabs
- 14-16 garlic cloves, crushed
- 3-4 dried red chillies, broken in half
- 2 tablespoons red chilli paste
- 2 tablespoons cornflour
- 4 tablespoons oil
- 2 stalks spring onion greens, chopped
- 1 tablespoon soy sauce
- 1 teaspoon sugar
- ¼ teaspoon MSG (optional)
- 1½ cups Fish or Chicken Stock (page 96 or 12)
- ½ teaspoon black peppercorns crushed
- salt to taste
- 2 tablespoons dry sherry (optional)
- 1 tablespoon vinegar
- 2 tablespoons sesame oil

Method

1 Separate claws and cut each crab into four pieces. Wash and remove gills

and stomach sac. Crack the claws lightly, wash thoroughly and drain well.

2 Mix cornflour with half a cup of water.

3 Heat oil in a wok or pan; add crushed garlic and red chillies and stir-fry for a few seconds. Add red chilli paste, soy sauce, sugar, MSG and the crabs. Continue to stir-fry for two or three minutes.

4 Stir in the stock and cook for two minutes, or until the crabs are cooked.

5 Stir in cornflour mixture and cook for one minute, or until the sauce thickens. Add crushed peppercorns, salt, dry sherry and vinegar.

6 Drizzle with sesame oil and serve hot, garnished with chopped spring onion greens.

FISH STOCK

Boil 200 grams fish bones, head, skin (any unutilised portions of fish), 5 cups of water, 1 sliced onion, 1 large button mushroom, 2-3 inch celery stalk, 1 bay leaf and 4-6 black peppercorns in a large pan.

Remove any scum, which floats to the top and simmer, for fifteen minutes.

Strain and use immediately.